Dear Claire & Brian

Wonderful to meet you.

Sheila

GW00725538

Looking for Lanterns

Sheila Payton

First published in 2015 by Flint Barn Publishing

British Library Cataloguing in Publication Data
A CIP record for this book is available from the British Library

ISBN: 978-0-9932176-0-9

Contents

*This selection of my poems is dedicated to the
memory of my mother
Helen Harriet Hensley Tindall*

Stone

Warm and washed,
smoothed by seas,
and now beachbathing
with his brothers.
No fight or flight
will hurry his heart.
Envied in submission,
lulled only by lapping
waves inching him to deeper
and still deeper peace.

Birth Certificate

On taking possession of the birth certificate of a mother I never knew.

To light a candle and illuminate my news,
its gold will hold a permanence however
temporary. You will be there in pure
unwhitened wax, I'll say your name
and wear the words.

First place my payment and collect
a candle, and if a clone exists I'll
lean my candle's wick to touch another's
lit. Secure it safely on the pyramid stand.

My leaving must be slow. I go
but cannot turn away, watching how
much longer you will shine.
I reach the door, rotate the iron ring
and now I am outside.

You stay within, and still are mine.

The Reading

Written after a poetry reading in an east Anglian church by Andrew Motion (then Poet Laureate).

You left the vestry blotting up blackness,
Forsaking safety, forsaking sanctuary,
With Siamese stealth you creamed the chancel
Reborn long limbed by the light of the lectern
To us with heads lifted expectant in pews.

You engaged and we listened
Loving your simpleness
Expressive gestures humble but bright,
Smiled as you disturbed, misplaced
    your poems
Shuffled them, shifted, laughed and then
    found.

You, you Adonis tousled haired Laureate,
Clad all in black offsetting gold curls,
You still the child when you spoke of your
    mother
Still curtaining your panes but never your
    heart.

Mother

Dead.
Before I knew her,
Saw her face,
Drew her comfort.

Dead.
Before I called her,
Showed her pictures,
Daisy heads.

Why mourn, when now its morning.
Why whisper, time has come to speak.

Masquerade

I wore the mask you made me,
tied it with a ring of gold,
laid it round an arch of diamonds
changed until I matched your mould.
Screened me from the heat of summer
barred my face from chilling rain,
laughed with gin and tonic through it,
shrank invisible from pain.
Stretch the mask and smother features,
shelter fawnly in cashmere,
shelter from the sight of slaughter,
shelter from the smell of fear.

Suffolk

Weary it seemed,
Life was a race,
Gathering pace……..
Then Suffolk in spring,
Green damp with promise,
Mellow cottages, round reed thatch,
Lime haze on hawthorn,
Birdsong sweet music
Rooks in the tall trees feathering nests.

Chamfered and worn,
Now glad to be born.

Channel

I'm trying to escape,
I'm chiselling a channel
Just wide enough to hide,
Lay blinkered, blind inside.
I'll plug my ears
And try to think again.
Inside my brain
A heaving mass
Of toiling ants
Will cease their work.
The cranking wheel
No longer turn,
Their crazed activity will calm
And one by one
They'll drop and die.

Then in the quiet,
Thoughts queuing up
May slowly be allowed,
With muffled tread,
To make their bed
Inside my head.
Or hang themselves on hooks.

Divorce

Shrouded in cool sheets
with sleep distancing itself ever further,
sifting through sand, decisions decided
upon, then disbanded with a changing
wind smarting our vision and dulling
our resolve.
There was so little time if we
were being timed.

We lay like beaten birds
blown from free flight,
beaten from their bracken covers,
beaten until feathers flew,
discarded now when lead
hangs heavy in our hearts.
The shoot had won the day,
trophies tied to a truck,
essential by some to be seen.

Silently sand slips through fingers
firm, once resolute, yet cannot contain
the slide, a landslide, and so it slips,
once started gathers speed and soon is spent.
Pale empty palms resigned to love's short run,
still questioning sand's speed.

Love

His eyes I love, his eyes so kind.
For granted surely there to find
A heart so strong, and yet know tears,
I've gazed those eyes a thousand years.

Or so it seems without his face,
His constant care, his steady pace,
Familiar, faithful, search and see,
My second self, the other me.

We've weathered life and firm sand found,
To form a peace, a common ground,
Of understanding, great good will,
I've loved you long – I love you still.

Pure Gold

Though love may dim and steal away,
How wrong we were to think could stay
Unchanged for thirty, forty years,
Of constancy we had no fears.

Such different people have we grown,
To choose again had we but known
How time effects it's artful will,
With all my heart I'd choose you still.

Don't agonise or reasons find,
Be patient and forever kind,
We need to fly – fly to be free,
Then winging home your face to see.

Night

Ebony envoy of the day,
How dark the night.
Distant stars beyond our reason,
Add heavenly height to earth.
Greet with gladness
The greatness of the night.

Dark velvet,
Comforting and calming,
Black is beauty,
Black is balm,
Fools would crave eternal brightness,
Longed for, lasting night.

Be a Man

Edward you just be
the man and I'll be the
fairy princess, dancing
in the circus, swinging
on the trapeze.

Just be the man Edward.

I'll wear pink satin shoes
and point "good toes
not naughty toes"
Miss Emily says!

No Edward you're the man
don't speak.

I'll open up my mirror box
and sprinkle me with stars.

Hush Edward – no don't speak
you aren't here yet
I'll tell you when you are.

I'll tell you Edward.

You're the man.

A House at war

A short sleep
Then war is waged on this house again
Wallpaper peels in rebellion,
Carpets curl their lips and snarl.

Silence is a long forgotten dream.
Serge suited thoughts march
Along our landing, leaving their
Unattended luggage, gathering suspicion
That even gentle spiders will not touch.

War has been waged and the ink of
Declaration has run through the rooms.
We have become expert at blotting
But cannot stop signatures becoming blurred
It's happening all the time.

War has been waged and rain is coming
Through the roof, we lay looking at the sky
But miss the stars. We have been robbed.
Bullets that should deafen have found silent
        targets
Shattering our ceilings and our sensibilities.

The stairs are scant protection,
Failing to separate floors
Downtrodden by night trampers
Who have found bedding overpowering
And sleep impossible.

By morning lens have been tampered with,
Distorted enemies march in finding us tired,
We smell their scent; it stays in full light.
This war is of a new order.
No banging of taps or shaking of pipes.

The furniture is solid but for how long?
Velvet and silk are crumpled and discarded
A craving has been created for straw floors,
White daub and wattle walls.

Call for the chaplain, call now but be careful,
His comfort will not come this time.
He can read to you, but the pages are
    scorched
By the words and punctuated by heated poker.

Pattern Repeat

I keep on walking up
When the stairs are
Moving down

I wake in the country
While my head is
Tuned to town

The flora that surrounds
Prematurely
Turns to brown

While the water
Flows serene
And is free.

Habit

Some fifteen years ago
You trod our unmade lane,
Which by construction
Could have been the barren land,

Had it not rained
So much that summer,
Your sandals were for desert wear
Not all terrain.

A leather belt drew in
Your heavy habit,
Above Christ crucified
Hung loose round your neck.

Now in advancing years
You introduce us to your sisters,
We share a convent meal
And laugh together when you tell them
I'm a super cook.

To listening nuns,
You talk in graphic glory
Of our space age 'sixties' cooker,
It's glass top hob
The only one you'd ever seen.

You seem too close to heaven
To meet with halogen.

The Long Watch

"Ash on an old man's sleeve is all the ash the burnt roses leave".
                                                    T. S. Elliott

His dressing gown grown old with him,
maroon and corded, condemned to cover
his scraggy manhood.

His watch is long and silent. No longer
        searching,
a cigarette his saviour, and satisfied by tea,
        another
night returns to day.

She was his spring his summer,
his aconite his primrose,
his morning star his evening dew.

She knows that he is there.
She needs him to let her lie
behind her lids and hear him breathe.

Missing

The jigsaw piece is furred
and will not fit
I'm tired of easing cardboard
cut-outs into foreboding spaces

"Can I be on the edge" I cry
"an edge piece with just one
safe side"
"All spaces there are spoken
for" they say,

but in another world
I'm waited for
my blanket aired
my place kept warm
the key has never turned
and time has never told.

Clearing house

Ladles of laughter
Scooped from the
Clearing house floor
Spilling and giggling
Through the gaps
Of our fingers

Then canned for long life
And packed
In the dark canvas
Depths of our bags
With ringpulls
Unruptured

We could open the cans
Whenever we wanted to
And a high kicking
Chorus would erupt
We never considered
Corrosion

With age we fear the
Cans may blow.

Sea Change

Breach the gap of generation,
Damn torrential expectation,
Rollercoasting deafening breakers,
Grab the thrills, the spills, be takers,
Thundering waves below to hide,
Tender sensitive inside.

Cast adrift with limpets clinging,
Sebaceous ocean seaweed bringing
Confiscation of free will,
Unfettered growth salt cannot still.
Buffetted urchins now collected,
All sounds familar neglected.

Search until the shoal is found,
Gaining depth, dark, where man is drowned,
Without a backward glance or wave
Bright fish are found, he is their slave
For one full season till its wain,
His desperate wish, acceptance gain.

With summer seas so turns the tide,
Calmer waters opening wide
To warm lagoons and tranquil shore,
And self destructive thoughts no more
Pervade his every wakening move,
He is sea changed, his worth has proved.

Wind Farm

Turning a corner, I see six of you
standing sentinel along the skyline,
your manx arms flailing wildly
in the wind.

Unchoreographed yet holding centre
stage, denied nature's anonymity.
Are you a twentieth century chorus line?

Or cork screws winding in the
wind, attempting to extract
earth's core?

Sea side

'It's dead' they say
'It's had its day'.

But no one told the waves
to fold their fury,
from next Sunday not to
seep upon the sand,
told the stones to
change their colour
then appear as one another,
no one stopped the clouds
from dappling sea and land.
No one told the spaniel
to stop chasing, and tire of
tugging tangled salted twine,
told the seagulls not to circle,
told the ocean not to sparkle.
Not to find the far horizon line.

Sloane Square

Disappearing underground
down through cream tiled
tunnel walls
Surging forward, people joining,
a mass forming.

The train sucks to a stop,
releases a soft sigh
and opens wide its side.
The mass now reinvents itself,
and fluid fills the vessel.
No drop is left behind.

Doors yawn, draw breath and
close on cue.

Eight stops to go, a tick each time
study form, then squint
along the route.
The punter
has a personal interest to
complete the course on time.

Next stop Sloane Square.
Now up and standing
under starter's orders,
waiting for the gate to clear.

November 11th

Armistice grey,
Remembrance day,
Long lonely beach,
Far reaching bay.
Grim rolling waves,
Dead Heroes' graves,
Chilled to the bone,
Longing for home.
As were the brave,
Memories save,
Lives lost in vain.
No man will gain,
Glory in war.
Glory no more!

Awakening

Days slowly lengthening, days feeling warmer,
White snow drops peeping precious and pure.
Strong daffodils shooting shouting bright greetings,
First sign of aconites first sign of spring.

Walks in the woodland
With wagging dogs waiting,
Waiting for sticks thrown again and again,
Fir cones in plenty and waxed pockets bulging,
Church in the distance
Striking the hour.

Holly

With us for just sixteen years.
Human in a canine cast,
but better.

The day she died she washed and
cleared our young dog's ears,
her daily duty, but on that day
with driven determination,

As if to leave this world in order,
as a mother mends and bakes before
a birth.

Her instinct trawled through evolution
and now acted out by dog approaching
death. An instinct still with man
through his sophistication.

We knew her soul, her bravery
through breathless panic, her
patience as she matched our
pace with deference.

She wasn't yours, she wasn't mine,
nor the children's, nor the children's
children's.

We were her's.

Gypsies

Unmistakable their horses, with rusty
chains, banishing all thoughts of bolting.
They bear restriction with broad
backed acceptance.

Romanies, ridged up against the hawthorn
bordering the common, their campfire
damped by drizzle that persists by day
and then trails off into mist by morning.

Green tarpaulin parlours, taut beneath
the never light November sky, with heavy
washing, waiting on a rope wrapped
around two trees.

Joy on survival

Focusing on one hair
of a pre metamorphic moth.

An anthill atomized
to an ant.

Lavender pared to
one sprig's cuckoo spit.

A deluge distilled
to a dewdrop.

Myself, stripped to the
single silk thread
of this thought.

Fly away Peter

From my safe chair
I stare, I'm there
with him.
I see the hostess
semaphore escape
to him.

I check the flaps
and feel the roar,
the no turn back.

I watch the clock
and at the hour
I fly with him.

Sandalwood

An eastern analgesic
softening sounds,
wreathing saltpetre
strands around our heads
each languid strand claiming
length, then disappearing
to be reborn as soft ash.

And now again new curls
are born and burn.

Imaging

Imaging and dispelling,
Encircling and quelling,
Gentle chanting in my head.
Tender green on mossy bed.
Soothing now surrounding.

Waving field in summer air,
Champimg cows consoling care,
Doddering grass on brown damp peat,
Frailest harebell to my feet,
Covering now containing.

Sombre shades their distance stay,
Vivid voices peaceful lay,
Cymbals, give triangles play.
Fashion flint to feather.

Lavender Cottage

I wouldn't derange it
Arrange it or change it,
Disturb it refurbish
Freshen or lessen it.

I'd continue to litter it,
Lessen the bitter bit.
Her hearth of flowers
On cinnamon ash.

I'd prove in it, move in it,
End of the day in it,
Stay in it pray in it
Lie down and live.

Sonata

Swaying in a summer
breeze, each grass
turns to interpret
music, breathed by the
baton wind.

All heads in harmony
non too tall too small,
bent low in sequence,
blown in an unscripted
silver roll, benignly
favouring earth's floor.
A benediction blown by a
billowing God.

She plays an ageless
slow sonata, taken
from some timeless score.
Soul's manuscript unheard
by man.

In Print

So is this it
The manuscript completed.
With living moments
Dead between its leaves.
Recorded life
Bound strong in hardback?

At the beginning
Bold and certain
Thoughts clear,
Along determined lines
Time dogged,
Earmarking corners,
Staggered sentence
And confused its style.

So is this it,
Or can we bulge
The binding further?
Expand forgetting
Anorexic days when airmail
Was preferred to parchment,
Those tissue paper days.

Youth will follow on
Inspiring further chapters,
Word tumbling over word
To have its say.
And laughing say
Our effort was mere practice,
A simple draft,
An exercise
Penned in a day.

Common Land

Home across the common,
watching the setting sun
squeezing blood orange
from its heart.

Trailing it through the sky
and finding its resting place
behind bonsai trees
blown bare on the far edge.

Now into the second bite
of our century we count
each sunset.

Words

Give me round words,
safe and sound words,
words that give
never take,
love to speak words,
brushing cheek words.
Words that bend
never break.

Cover high words,
smother die words,
words that shout
harsh or sly,
tinder dark words,
swim from shark words.
Words may weep
never cry.

Black

Black was his colour
Black the size of night
He covered light
He turned light inside out
And curled up
In it's lining.

Black was his mentor
And his minder.

The Box

Fingering man's marquetry,
I take possesion and the deed is done.
Sweet seed pearls, smocked silk lining,
Treasures unknown, a heart laid bare.
Columned death torn from a newsprint page,
A curl of golden hair, grown tarnished
now with age. Jerome photograph tinted
with time …. a valentine. Fond personal
mix, parts of a pocket watch, Testament
text, a crucifix.
To have her back,
To ask her why and when,
Her eyes she never dried.
Oh yes – she cried.

Kitchen Whisk

Poem 1

My wands of steel
stretch high and bend
meticulously spaced
back fall to base
bound for security
larger and I could
house a small bird
for you
just now
I am
a cage
without a perch
without a hatch
without a hen
or then
a slim balloon
sailing soon
without a basket
needing helium
heading nowhere.

Poem 2

I'm told to write of
wirey strands
whisking air and
agitating eggs
instead
I'd rather write of birds
"I'll fill your house with wild birds
and they will sing for
you"

Dust To Dust

See the boy in the lift, high rising home,
A key round his neck, a noose loosely waiting.
No 'Mum it's me' to an empty room,
With it's greedy machine
Mindlessly waiting to gobble his video.
We lead him to white powder.

His hair crudely cut round his forty year face,
Long tongued trainers for the race.
Does he care? He doesn't dare.
If only, if only someone was there.
We push him to white powder

He leaves the flat, down to the square,
Buggies pass, and used men stare into the future.
He knows the place, and buys a drink,
Then kicks around the can.
Boys from nowhere join him fast,
Survivor? Well, his mould is cast!
We'll kill him with white powder.

Dragon fly

We lived for the spring of earth, freedom,
release and rest,
a gradual descent to familiar ground.

Now looking down like dazed dragonflies,
still capable of strength and single
mindedness,
our task once was to turn on command
and cover crippled cargo.

Live days are numbered now. Wings once
a-whirr with speed
mourn their velocity, like planes stacking,
waiting for the all clear.

Once, heady at high altitude, misreading a
signal,
gratefully we glided down, only to be recalled.

We will obey now. Stack and circle,
stack and circle, stack and circle
until fuel fails.

Her's

The herbs were her's.
She planted them
in servant's sinks
around her yard.
Lovingly she fingered
lemon balm, with
lowered lids drew strength
from feverfew.

He would allow a
sprig of mint
into his bed,
But found no majesty
in fennel, no sanctuary
in heartsease.
But watered wigwammed beans
To dwarf nextdoor's.

The Room

The happiest place I've ever known,
A cluttered room, where I have grown
To dearly love the joy of home,
Abandon shoes, no thought to roam.

Books bind its walls, their brackets sag,
Shelves and sheet music, still in bag
From days of practice and despair,
But always dogs and Dad were there.

Musty, fusty, velvety gold,
So rarely drawn with faded fold,
Small square panes with moisture dripping,
Logs in grate alive and spitting.

Sinking deep in glorious feather,
Life may change, but memories never,
Longingly I would recreate
Worn comfort of my childhood state.

The Barn

Dust has settled in the sitting room
And left behind a stillness.
A shy powder has softened even
Hard wood.

Nothing has been disturbed for days.
Papers dropped beside a chair may
Fear the heavyweights of Sunday,
But space will be found for them.

We sit, wood pigeon's call
Coming down, down through the
Chimney to where the ash and parburned
Candles wait for another night.

This room has retired,
Deserving dust and dreams.
The dog has found comfort
Curled up in a corner content.